Accelerated Christian Training Series

Laying the FOUNDATION

BOOK 4

FROM COVENANT TO KINGDOM

Dr. Mark Hanby

© Copyright 2001 — Mark Hanby Ministries

All rights reserved. This book is protected by the copyright laws of the United States of America. This book may not be copied or reprinted for commercial gain or profit. The use of short quotations or occasional page copying for personal or group study is permitted and encouraged. Permission will be granted upon request. Unless otherwise identified, Scripture quotations are from the New King James Version of the Bible. Emphasis within Scripture quotations is the author's own. Please note that Destiny Image's publishing style capitalizes certain pronouns in Scripture that refer to the Father, Son, and Holy Spirit, and may differ from some Bible publishers' styles.

Take note that the name satan and related names are not capitalized. We choose not to acknowledge him, even to the point of violating grammatical rules.

Destiny Image® Publishers, Inc.
P.O. Box 310
Shippensburg, PA 17257-0310

"Speaking to the Purposes of God for This
Generation and for the Generations to Come"

ISBN 0-7684-2145-4

For Worldwide Distribution
Printed in the U.S.A.

This book and all other Destiny Image, Revival Press,
MercyPlace, Fresh Bread, Destiny Image Fiction,
and Treasure House books are available
at Christian bookstores and distributors worldwide.

For a U.S. bookstore nearest you, call **1-800-722-6774**.
For more information on foreign distributors,
call **717-532-3040**.
Or reach us on the Internet: **www.destinyimage.com**

Contents

	Introduction	5
I.	**Taking Possession of the Promises of God**	10

    A.   By What Right Did the Nation of Israel Take Possession of the Land of Canaan?
    B.   What Did Israel Have to Do in Order to Take Possession of Their Inheritance?
    C.   Did Israel Obey God Under Joshua and Take Possession of the Land God Promised?
    D.   How Did God Respond to the Disobedience of the People of Israel?
    E.   Who Was Samuel?

II.	**Establishing the Kingdom**	20

    A.   Who Did the Lord Intend to Rule Over the Nation of Israel?
    B.   How Did the Lord Respond to Israel's Desire for an Earthly King?
    C.   Who Was Saul?
    D.   Who Was David? What Was His Relationship to God?
    E.   What Was God's Promise to King David and How Did It Come to Pass?
    F.   What Was the Spiritual Significance of David's Reign?
    G.   Who Was Solomon? What Was His Relationship to God?
    H.   What Was the Result of Solomon's Failing Before God?
    I.   Why and How Did God Allow the Nation of Israel to Be Destroyed?
    J.   How Did the Issues of Faith and Obedience Enter Into the Fate of Israel?

III.	**The Message of the Prophets**	40

    A.   What Is a Prophet?
    B.   Who Were the Prophets of the Old Testament?

	C.	What Rules Must We Follow in Order to Understand the Words of the Prophets?
	D.	What Was the Mission of the Prophets?
	E.	What Was the Message of the Prophets?
	F.	What Did the Prophets Say Concerning Jesus Christ?
	G.	What Was the Message of the Prophets Concerning the Church?
IV.	**Restoring the Remnant of Israel** **59**
	A.	For What Purpose Did God Preserve a Remnant of Israel?
	B.	How Did God Preserve the Remnant of Israel?
	C.	Who Did God Choose to Lead This Remnant? What Were Their Roles?
	D.	What Was the Opposition That the Returning Remnant Faced As They Rebuilt Jerusalem?
	E.	What Lessons Can Be Learned From the Return of the Remnant?
	F.	What Meaning Does the Restoration of the Remnant Hold for Us Today?

Introduction

And you shall know the truth, and the truth shall make you free (John 8:32).

What Is Truth?

Truth Is a Person

"What is truth?" Pilate asked Jesus (Jn. 18:38). The answer to Pilate's timeless question was standing before him. Truth is not a series of facts or the sum of information. Truth is a Person: Jesus Christ. Jesus said of Himself, "I am the way, the truth, and the life" (Jn. 14:6). Truth is not only rational, it is relational. Religious theory that only teaches about God can never liberate the soul. True freedom is found in knowing Him. "And ye shall know the truth, and the truth shall make you free" (Jn. 8:32).

God has chosen to unfold His relational truth in various ways throughout the Bible and always in the form of personal relationship between Himself and men such as Adam, Noah, and Abraham. The unfolding revelation of God's relationship with man was spelled out in agreements between God and man called covenants. What better way to unfold a relational truth than in the context of relationship?

Truth Is the Result of Seeking Jesus

This relational truth is more than experience. Despite his great experience on the road to Damascus, the apostle Paul did not end his search for truth but wrote, "...that I may know *Him* and the power of His resurrection, and the fellowship of His sufferings..." (Phil. 3:10, emphasis mine). Job, wounded and in distress, cried out, "Oh that I knew where I might find *Him*..."

(Job 23:3). Jesus said, "Blessed are those who hunger and thirst for righteousness, for they shall be filled" (Mt. 5:6). Our finding the truth is the result of a hunger to know the Person of Jesus Christ. We do not seek truth and find Jesus; we seek Jesus and find the truth.

Truth Is a Highway

We may think of truth as a highway—an endless journey into the Person of God. All of us walking in the light of relationship with God are at some point in that journey. As we "seek the Lord" and "search the Scriptures," we advance. The **A**ccelerated **C**hristian **T**raining **S**eries has been created to help us move on in that journey into the Lord regardless of whether we are new believers or seasoned saints of God. There is always more truth for us regardless of our place along the road. "His ways [are] past finding out" (Rom. 11:33b).

It is important that every believer follow a course such as this. Although the believer may be exposed to a variety of good biblical preaching, there must be a systematic seeking after truth to provide a foundation upon which to grow in relationship with the Person of Jesus. Imagine agreeing to marry someone of whom you had only seen a pencil sketching. It is our intention in this course of seeking to paint a full and vital portrait of the Christ who is alive in you.

If you are a new traveler on the highway of truth, you have begun the most exciting journey of your life. Many parallels can be drawn between the new believer and a newborn child. It would be a criminal act to leave an infant out in the cold or in a house without someone to give him attention and care. It is likewise a tragedy when the Church does not nurture newborn Christians. If newborns are going to be healthy and grow to

Introduction

maturity, they must be carefully and loving fed with the truth of the word.

Truth Brings Maturity

The Christian life is a "growing up into Him in all things...until we come to the measure of the stature of the fullness of Christ" (see Eph. 4:13-15). It is important that we place ourselves under pastoral care if we are to "grow up." Even Jesus, who astonished the doctors and lawyers of His time, was entrusted to His parents' care. The Bible says, "Obey thse who rule over you, and be submissive: for they watch out for your souls" (Heb. 13:17). To reject the care of pastoral oversight is to reject God's plan to bring us to Himself and to leave ourselves open to error and the exit from the highway of our journey into the truth.

The ministry that God has given to the Church is five-phased with a threefold purpose. Ephesians 4:11 tells us that God has placed in the church apostles, prophets, evangelists, pastors and teachers. Their purpose is to mature, feed and motivate believers in their own calling and ministry. Only when this equipping is established in the life of the believer will they progress from spiritual newborn to spiritual childhood and on to spiritual adulthood.

In the life of every Christian there must come a point where we "put away childish things" (1 Cor. 13:11). As we become "rooted and grounded" in the basic principles of faith we are "no more children, tossed to and fro, and carried about with every wind of doctrine" (Eph. 4:14). As we grow and mature in the faith we are able to rise above our own problems and trials and reach out with power and confidence to minister the truth to the needs of those around us.

How the Accelerated Christian Training Series Works

The **A**ccelerated **C**hristian **T**raining **S**eries has been designed to meet the crucial need for intensive training in the basic doctrines of the Christian faith. These doctrines are revealed in the context of relationship between God and man. It is designed as a self-instruction course in which believers can journey at their own pace. You will find review questions at the end of each section of material you have studied that will help you to retain what you've learned.

There is an exercise called "Dig a Little Deeper; Grow a Little Closer" at the end of each major section. These reflective questions are designed to help you synthesize the truths you have been taught and then apply them in a personal way. You will be invited to journal throughout the study of this book to provide you with a record of your new understanding and growth in God. Journaling will help you to grow in your ability to hear God's voice and adjust your life and understanding to His purpose.

Following this **A.C.T.S.** course will stimulate and accelerate your spiritual understanding and bring you to a more intimate knowledge of the Truth, who is Jesus Christ. We pray that you will grow in the awareness of the Lord's presence as He guides you to Himself through the study of His Word.

Two Companions for the Road

During this time of new growth in your spiritual life there will be questions that come to mind. You will meet two companions throughout this series on the road to truth. They are Newly Newborn and Truly Taughtright. Newly will ask some of the same questions that you ask, and Truly, his mentor, will give the answers.

Introduction

From Covenant to Kingdom

Imagine that you learn you are the heir of a great fortune and all you have to do is to show up and take possession of it. But somehow on the way to claiming your newfound wealth, you are distracted by something you find attractive in a store window. You stop to look at some bauble and completely miss the meeting at which you were to be made rich with money to buy something of much more value than what captivated you in the store window. For the sake of trash you forsook a great inheritance.

That is essentially the story we will encounter with Israel. God promised them an inheritance far beyond anything they could ever ask or think, but they took their eyes off of His promised inheritance and lost it. How would God restore them? The great treasure was in reality a life of rest in God. It would be a life characterized by an intimate contact with God who desired to dwell among His people. God Himself was in fact the great fortune they were to inherit. How many times do we trade what is of true and eternal value for that which is destined for moth and rust? Let's see how God begins to reveal his plan for restoration.

I. Taking Possession of the Promises of God

A. By What Right Did the Nation of Israel Take Possession of the Land of Canaan?

1. Israel took possession by virtue of the promises made by God to their father Abraham.

Then the Lord appeared to Abram and said, "To your descendants I will give this land." And there he built an altar to the Lord, who had appeared to him (Genesis 12:7).

Also I give to you and your descendants after you the land in which you are a stranger, all the land of Canaan, as an everlasting possession; and I will be their God (Genesis 17:8).

2. Israel took possession by the confirmation of God's promise through Moses.

See, I have set the land before you; go in and possess the land which the Lord swore to your fathers—to Abraham, Isaac, and Jacob—to give to them and their descendants after them (Deuteronomy 1:8).

Then the Lord said to Moses, "Depart and go up from here, you and the people whom you have brought out of the land of Egypt, to the land of which I swore to Abraham, Isaac, and Jacob, saying, 'To your descendants I will give it'" (Exodus 33:1).

3. Israel took possession of the land as an inheritance from God.

You shall follow what is altogether just, that you may live and inherit the land which the Lord your God is giving you (Deuteronomy 16:20).

B. What Did Israel Have to Do in Order to Take Possession of Their Inheritance?

1. To take possession of their inheritance Israel had to have faith in God's word and provision.

Every place that the sole of your foot will tread upon I have given you, as I said to Moses...Be strong and of good courage, for to this people you shall divide as an inheritance the land which I swore to their fathers to give them (Joshua 1:3,6).

2. To take possession of their inheritance Israel had to obey leaders that God placed ahead of them.

"Let the Lord, the God of the spirits of all flesh, set a man over the congregation, who may go out before them and go in before them, who may lead them out and bring them in, that the congregation of the Lord may not be like sheep which have no shepherd." And the Lord said to Moses: "Take Joshua the son of Nun with you, a man in whom is the Spirit, and lay your hand on him" (Numbers 27:16-18).

After the death of Moses the servant of the Lord, it came to pass that the Lord spoke to Joshua the son of Nun, Moses' assistant, saying: "Moses My servant is dead. Now therefore, arise, go over this Jordan, you and all this people, to the land which I am giving to them—the children of Israel" (Joshua 1:1-2).

3. To take possession of their inheritance Israel renewed the covenant with God through the sign of circumcision.

At that time the Lord said to Joshua, "Make flint knives for yourself, and circumcise the sons of Israel again the second time." So Joshua made flint knives for himself, and circumcised the sons of Israel at the hill of the foreskins. And this is the reason why Joshua circumcised them: All the people who came out of Egypt who were males, all the men of war, had died in the wilderness on the way, after they had come out of Egypt. For all the people who came out had been circumcised, but all the people born in the wilderness, on the way as they came out of Egypt, had not been circumcised (Joshua 5:2-5).

4. To take possession of their inheritance Israel had to keep the law of God. There were blessings for obedience and curses for disobedience of the law.

Only be strong and very courageous, that you may observe to do according to all the law which Moses My servant commanded you; do not turn from it to the right hand or to the left, that you may prosper wherever you go (Joshua 1:7).

Behold, I set before you today a blessing and a curse: the blessing, if you obey the commandments of the Lord your God which I command you today; and the curse, if you do not obey the commandments of the Lord your God, but turn aside from the way which I command you today, to go after other gods which you have not known (Deuteronomy 11:26-28).

C. **Did Israel Obey God Under Joshua and Take Possession of the Land God Promised?**

   1. Israel obeyed God all the days of Joshua's leadership. God gave them all the land He had promised to their fathers.

Israel served the Lord all the days of Joshua, and all the days of the elders who outlived Joshua, who had known all the works of the Lord which He had done for Israel (Joshua 24:31).

   2. Israel took possession of all the land that God promised.

So the Lord gave to Israel all the land of which He had sworn to give to their fathers, and they took possession of it and dwelt in it. The Lord gave them rest all around, according to all that He had sworn to their fathers. And not a man of all their enemies stood against them; the Lord delivered all their enemies into their hand. Not a word failed of any good thing which the Lord had spoken to the house of Israel. All came to pass (Joshua 21:43-45).

   3. Israel obeyed the law of God until after the death of Joshua.

Now Joshua the son of Nun, the servant of the Lord, died when he was one hundred and ten years old...When all that generation had been gathered to their fathers, another generation arose after them who did not know the Lord nor the work which He had done for Israel. Then the children of Israel did evil in the sight of the Lord, and served the Baals; and they forsook the Lord God of their fathers, who had brought them out of the land of Egypt; and they followed other gods from among the gods of the people who were all around them, and they bowed down to them; and they provoked the Lord to anger (Judges 2:8,10-12).

D. How Did God Respond to the Disobedience of the People of Israel?

1. God responded to their disobedience by giving them over to the heathen nations whose gods they served.

And the anger of the Lord was hot against Israel. So He delivered them into the hands of plunderers who despoiled them; and He sold them into the hands of their enemies all around, so that they could no longer stand before their enemies. Wherever they went out, the hand of the Lord was against them for calamity, as the Lord had said, and as the Lord had sworn to them. And they were greatly distressed (Judges 2:14-15).

2. God responded to their disobedience by showing Israel grace and mercy when they cried out to Him. He raised up judges who delivered them from the hand of their enemies.

Nevertheless, the Lord raised up judges who delivered them out of the hand of those who plundered them (Judges 2:16).

Therefore You delivered them into the hand of their enemies, who oppressed them; and in the time of their trouble, when they cried to You, You heard from heaven; and according to Your abundant mercies You gave them deliverers who saved them from the hand of their enemies (Nehemiah 9:27).

And for their sake He remembered His covenant, and relented according to the multitude of His mercies (Psalm 106:45).

3. God responded to their disobedience by sending them prophets to remind them of their relationship with God.

E. **Who Was Samuel?**

1. Samuel was the last "judge" of Israel and the first in the line of prophets.

And all Israel from Dan to Beersheba knew that Samuel had been established as a prophet of the Lord (1 Samuel 3:20).

And Samuel judged Israel all the days of his life (1 Samuel 7:15).

2. Samuel heard the complaints of the people who wanted a king like the other nations around them had. Samuel was displeased with their request.

From Covenant to Kingdom

> *Then all the elders of Israel gathered together and came to Samuel at Ramah, and said to him, "Look, you are old, and your sons do not walk in your ways. Now make us a king to judge us like all the nations"* (1 Samuel 8:4-5).

3. The Lord used Samuel to set up the kingdom of Israel. It was Samuel who anointed the first two kings of Israel.

> *Then Samuel explained to the people the behavior of royalty, and wrote it in a book and laid it up before the Lord. And Samuel sent all the people away, every man to his house.* (1 Samuel 10:25).

Let's Review What We Have Learned About Possessing the Promises of God.

1. Israel took possession (of the land) by virtue of the _____ made by God to their father Abraham.

2. Israel took possession of the land as an _____ from God.

3. If Israel was to possess all that God had for them it would require these two things: _____ and _____. (Hint: They are the same two things that Abraham demonstrated.)

4. To take possession of their inheritance Israel had to keep the _____ of God. There were _____ for obedience to the law and _____ for disobedience.

5. Israel took possession of _____ the land that God promised.

Taking Possession of the Promises of God

6. Israel obeyed the _____ of God until after the _____ of Joshua.

7. God responded to Israel's disobedience by showing them _____ and _____ when they cried out to Him.

8. Samuel was the last _____ of Israel and the first in the line of _____.

Dig a Little Deeper; Grow a Little Closer

1. Read the following verses and respond to the questions that follow.

Israel served the Lord all the days of Joshua, and all the days of the elders who outlived Joshua, who had known all the works of the Lord which He had done for Israel (Joshua 24:31).

Now Joshua the son of Nun, the servant of the Lord, died when he was one hundred and ten years old. And they buried him within the border of his inheritance at Timnath Heres, in the mountains of Ephraim, on the north side of Mount Gaash. When all that generation had been gathered to their fathers, another generation arose after them who did not know the Lord nor the work which He had done for Israel. Then the children of Israel did evil in the sight of the Lord, and served the Baals (Judges 2:8-11).

2. During whose lifetimes did Israel serve the Lord according to these verses?

3. Based on what these verses say, what do you see as the leading factor in Israel's falling away from God?

4. What do these events say to you about the importance of teaching the law and the knowledge of God to the next generation? What will result if we fail to do so?

Review Notes

II. Establishing the Kingdom

A. Who Did the Lord Intend to Rule Over the Nation of Israel?

1. The Lord Himself was to be the King over Israel. It is the Lord who is King over all those who have submitted themselves to His reign.

But Gideon said to them, "I will not rule over you, nor shall my son rule over you; the Lord shall rule over you" (Judges 8:23).

For the Lord is our Judge, the Lord is our Lawgiver, the Lord is our King; he will save us (Isaiah 33:22).

For God is my King from of old, working salvation in the midst of the earth (Psalm 74:12).

O Israel, you are destroyed, but your help is from Me. I will be your King; where is any other, that he may save you in all your cities? And your judges to whom you said, "Give me a king and princes"? (Hosea 13:9-10)

2. But Israel rejected the Lord who was to reign as King. They wanted a king of flesh like the nations around them had. They said that Samuel was too old and that his sons did not follow the Lord.

Then all the elders of Israel gathered together and came to Samuel at Ramah, and said to him, "Look, you are old, and your sons do not walk in your ways. Now make us a king to judge us like all the nations." But the thing displeased Samuel when

Establishing the Kingdom

they said, "Give us a king to judge us." So Samuel prayed to the Lord (1 Samuel 8:4-6).

B. **How Did the Lord Respond to Israel's Desire for an Earthly King?**

1. The Lord was displeased at their request.

And the Lord said to Samuel, "Heed the voice of the people in all that they say to you; for they have not rejected you, but they have rejected Me, that I should not reign over them" (1 Samuel 8:7).

2. The Lord warned the nation that earthly kings were harsh and demanding. Nevertheless, Israel, with hardened hearts, rejected God. God's warning was fulfilled.

And he said..."He will take your sons...He will take your daughters...And he will take the best of your fields, your vineyards, and your olive groves...He will take a tenth of your grain and your vintage...And he will take your male servants, your female servants, your finest young men, and your donkeys, and put them to his work. He will take a tenth of your sheep. And you will be his servants. And you will cry out in that day because of your king whom you have chosen for yourselves, and the Lord will not hear you in that day" (1 Samuel 8:11-18).

Nevertheless the people refused to obey the voice of Samuel; and they said, "No, but we will have a king over us, that we also may be like all the nations, and that our king may judge us and go out before us and fight our battles" (1 Samuel 8:19-20).

Then the king answered the people roughly, and rejected the advice which the elders had given him; and he spoke to them according to the advice of the young men, saying, "My father made your yoke heavy, but I will add to your yoke; my father chastised you with whips, but I will chastise you with scourges!" (1 Kings 12:13-14)

    3.   The Lord provided Saul to be king over the nation of Israel.

"Tomorrow about this time I will send you a man from the land of Benjamin, and you shall anoint him commander over My people Israel, that he may save My people from the hand of the Philistines; for I have looked upon My people, because their cry has come to Me." And when Samuel saw Saul, the Lord said to him, "There he is, the man of whom I spoke to you. This one shall reign over My people" (1 Samuel 9:16-17).

C. Who Was Saul?

    1.   Saul was the first king of Israel.

Then Samuel took a flask of oil and poured it on his head, and kissed him and said: "Is it not because the Lord has anointed you commander over His inheritance?" (1 Samuel 10:1)

So all the people went to Gilgal, and there they made Saul king before the Lord in Gilgal. There they made sacrifices of peace offerings before the Lord, and there Saul and all the men of Israel rejoiced greatly (1 Samuel 11:15).

Establishing the Kingdom

2. Saul walked with God in the beginning of his reign and was empowered by the Spirit of God.

Then the Spirit of the Lord will come upon you, and you will prophesy with them and be turned into another man. And let it be, when these signs come to you, that you do as the occasion demands; for God is with you (1 Samuel 10:6-7).

When they came there to the hill, there was a group of prophets to meet him; then the Spirit of God came upon him, and he prophesied among them (1 Samuel 10:10).

3. Saul sinned against the Lord as he tried to take the role of a priest.

Then he waited seven days, according to the time set by Samuel. But Samuel did not come to Gilgal...So Saul said, "Bring a burnt offering and peace offerings here to me." And he offered the burnt offering. Now it happened, as soon as he had finished presenting the burnt offering, that Samuel came; and Saul went out to meet him, that he might greet him. And Samuel said, "What have you done?" And Saul said, "When I saw that the people were scattered from me...you did not come ...The Philistines will now come down on me at Gilgal...I have not made supplication to the Lord." And Samuel said to Saul, "You have done foolishly. You have not kept the commandment of the Lord your God, which He commanded you. For now the Lord would have established your kingdom over Israel forever. But now your kingdom shall not continue. The Lord has sought for Himself a man after His own heart, and the Lord has commanded him to be commander" (1 Samuel 13:8-14).

4. Saul later failed to fully obey the word of the Lord through Samuel the prophet, and the Spirit as well as the kingdom was taken from him.

[Samuel said] *"Now go and attack Amalek, and utterly destroy all that they have"...But Saul and the people spared Agag and the best of the sheep, the oxen, the fatlings, the lambs, and all that was good, and were unwilling to utterly destroy them...But Samuel said..."Now the Lord sent you on a mission, and said, 'Go, and utterly destroy the sinners, the Amalekites, and fight against them until they are consumed.' Why then did you not obey the voice of the Lord?" And Saul said to Samuel, "But I have obeyed...But the people took of the plunder"...Then Samuel said: "Has the Lord as great delight in burnt offerings and sacrifices, as in obeying the voice of the Lord? Behold, to obey is better than sacrifice, and to heed than the fat of rams"...But Samuel said to Saul, "I will not return with you, for you have rejected the word of the Lord, and the Lord has rejected you from being king over Israel"* (1 Samuel 15:3,9,14,18-22,26).

5. Saul turned completely away from God. He sought counsel from witches and eventually died defeated, at his own hand.

Establishing the Kingdom

Then Saul said to his servants, "Find me a woman who is a medium, that I may go to her and inquire of her." And his servants said to him, "In that, there is a woman who is a medium at EnDor" (1 Samuel 28:7).

Then Saul said to his armorbearer, "Draw your sword, and thrust me through with it, lest these uncircumcised men come and thrust me through and abuse me." But his armorbearer would not, for he was greatly afraid. Therefore Saul took a sword and fell on it (1 Samuel 31:4).

D. Who Was David? What Was His Relationship to God?

    1. David was the least of the sons of Jesse—a shepherd whom God chose to succeed Saul as king over Israel.

Now the Lord said to Samuel, "How long will you mourn for Saul, seeing I have rejected him from reigning over Israel? Fill your horn with oil, and go; I am sending you to Jesse the Bethlehemite. For I have provided Myself a king among his sons" (1 Samuel 16:1).

Then Samuel took the horn of oil and anointed him in the midst of his brothers; and the Spirit of the Lord came upon David from that day forward. So Samuel arose and went to Ramah (1 Samuel 16:13).

He also chose David His servant, and took him from the sheepfolds; from following the ewes that had young He brought him, to shepherd Jacob His people, and Israel His inheritance. So he shepherded them according to the integrity of his heart, and guided them by the skillfulness of his hands (Psalm 78:70-72).

2. David was a "man after God's own heart." He would not be like Saul who served his own interests but would serve the Lord in faithfulness to see the kingdom reign of God established in Israel. David was a man of faith and obedience to the Lord.

But now your kingdom shall not continue. The Lord has sought for Himself a man after His own heart, and the Lord has commanded him to be commander over His people, because you have not kept what the Lord commanded you (1 Samuel 13:14).

Establishing the Kingdom

3. David was a worshiper of God at all times. He wrote many Psalms, which were and are used to praise the Lord.

Bless the Lord, O my soul; and all that is within me, bless His holy name! (Psalm 103:1)

Then David spoke to the Lord the words of this song, on the day when the Lord had delivered him from the hand of all his enemies, and from the hand of Saul. And he said: "The Lord is my rock and my fortress and my deliverer; the God of my strength, in whom I will trust; my shield and the horn of my salvation, my stronghold and my refuge; my Savior, You save me from violence. I will call upon the Lord, who is worthy to be praised; so shall I be saved from my enemies" (2 Samuel 22:1-4).

4. David was also a man who failed the Lord in sin but repented of his sin and was restored.

Then it happened one evening that David arose from his bed and walked on the roof of the king's house. And from the roof he saw a woman bathing, and the woman was very beautiful to behold...And he wrote in the letter, saying, "Set Uriah in the forefront of the hottest battle, and retreat from him, that he may be struck down and die." Then the men of the city came out and fought with Joab. And some of the people of the servants of David fell; and Uriah the Hittite died also. And when her mourning was over, David sent and brought her to his house, and she became his wife and bore him a son. But the thing that David had done displeased the Lord (2 Samuel 11:2,15,17,27).

So David said to Nathan, "I have sinned against the Lord." And Nathan said to David, "The Lord also has put away your sin; you shall not die" (2 Samuel 12:13).

E. What Was God's Promise to King David and How Did It Come to Pass?

1. God promised that He would establish the throne of David forever. This means that someone from his line would always sit on the throne of Israel.

And your house and your kingdom shall be established forever before you. Your throne shall be established forever (2 Samuel 7:16).

Once I have sworn by My holiness; I will not lie to David: His seed shall endure forever, and his throne as the sun before Me; It shall be established forever like the moon, even like the faithful witness in the sky (Psalm 89:35-37).

The Lord has sworn in truth to David; He will not turn from it: "I will set upon your throne the fruit of your body" (Psalm 132:11).

For thus says the Lord: "David shall never lack a man to sit on the throne of the house of Israel" (Jeremiah 33:17).

2. Even though David's descendants and Israel failed, God fulfilled His promise

through the Person of Jesus Christ, Son of David.

For unto us a Child is born, unto us a Son is given; and the government will be upon His shoulder. And His name will be called Wonderful, Counselor, Mighty God, Everlasting Father, Prince of Peace. Of the increase of His government and peace there will be no end, upon the throne of David and over His kingdom, to order it and establish it with judgment and justice from that time forward, even forever. The zeal of the Lord of hosts will perform this (Isaiah 9:6-7).

"Behold, the days are coming," says the Lord, "that I will raise to David a Branch of righteousness; a King shall reign and prosper, and execute judgment and righteousness in the earth (Jeremiah 23:5).

He will be great, and will be called the Son of the Highest; and the Lord God will give Him the throne of His father David. And He will reign over the house of Jacob forever, and of His kingdom there will be no end (Luke 1:32-33).

F. What Was the Spiritual Significance of David's Reign?

1. It was through David's reign that God prophetically revealed His spiritual purpose in Christ and in the Church. *David* is a prophetic name for Christ.

But they shall serve the Lord their God, and David their king, whom I will raise up for them (Jeremiah 30:9).

I will establish one shepherd over them, and he shall feed them—My servant David. He shall feed them and be their shepherd (Ezekiel 34:23).

2. David's lineage is referred to as his "house" or "tabernacle," which God promised to establish forever. It was through David's house that Jesus Christ, the Messiah, would be born.

Moreover I will appoint a place for My people Israel, and will plant them, that they may dwell in a place of their own and move no more; nor shall the sons of wickedness oppress them anymore, as previously, since the time that I commanded judges to be over My people Israel, and have caused you to rest from all your enemies. Also the Lord tells you that He will make you a house (2 Samuel 7:10-11).

For You, O Lord of hosts, God of Israel, have revealed this to Your servant, saying, "I will build you a house." Therefore Your servant has found it in his heart to pray this prayer to You (2 Samuel 7:27).

Men and brethren, let me speak freely to you of the patriarch David, that he is both dead and buried, and his tomb is with us to this day. Therefore, being a prophet, and knowing that God had sworn with an oath to him that of the fruit of his body, according to the flesh, He would raise up the

Christ to sit on his throne, he, foreseeing this, spoke concerning the resurrection of the Christ, that His soul was not left in Hades, nor did His flesh see corruption. This Jesus God has raised up, of which we are all witnesses (Acts 2:29-32).

Simon has declared how God at the first visited the Gentiles to take out of them a people for His name. And with this the words of the prophets agree, just as it is written: **"After this I will return and will rebuild the tabernacle of David, which has fallen down; I will rebuild its ruins, and I will set it up**; *so that the rest of mankind may seek the Lord, even all the Gentiles who are called by My name, says the Lord who does all these things"* (Acts 15:14-17).

G. **Who Was Solomon? What Was His Relationship to God?**

 1. Solomon was King David's son who became the third king of Israel.

Then Solomon sat on the throne of his father David; and his kingdom was firmly established (1 Kings 2:12).

Then Solomon sat on the throne of the Lord as king instead of David his father, and prospered; and all Israel obeyed him (1 Chronicles 29:23).

 2. Solomon was charged by God to build Him a great temple. The temple was to be a place where God's glory would dwell on earth.

And behold, I propose to build a house for the name of the Lord my God, as the Lord spoke to my father David, saying, "Your son, whom I will set on your throne in your place, he shall build the house for My name" (1 Kings 5:5).

And it came to pass, when the priests came out of the holy place, that the cloud filled the house of the Lord, so that the priests could not continue ministering because of the cloud; for the glory of the Lord filled the house of the Lord (1 Kings 8:10-11).

When Solomon had finished praying, fire came down from heaven and consumed the burnt offering and the sacrifices; and the glory of the Lord filled the temple (2 Chronicles 7:1).

3. Solomon failed God by taking wives from heathen nations and allowing them to bring their false gods.

For it was so, when Solomon was old, that his wives turned his heart after other gods; and his heart was not loyal to the Lord his God, as was the heart of his father David. For Solomon went after Ashtoreth the goddess of the Sidonians, and after Milcom the abomination of the Ammonites. Solomon did evil in the sight of the Lord, and did not fully follow the Lord, as did his father David (1 Kings 11:4-6).

H. What Was the Result of Solomon's Failing Before God?

1. Solomon's kingdom was taken from him and given to one who was not in David's

Establishing the Kingdom

line. However, God preserved a "remnant" of David's kingdom through which He would fulfill His promise to David.

Therefore the Lord said to Solomon, "Because you have done this, and have not kept My covenant and My statutes, which I have commanded you, I will surely tear the kingdom away from you and give it to your servant. Nevertheless I will not do it in your days, for the sake of your father David; I will tear it out of the hand of your son. However I will not tear away the whole kingdom; I will give one tribe to your son for the sake of my servant David, and for the sake of Jerusalem which I have chosen" (1 Kings 11:11-13).

2. After 120 years of unity, Israel was divided into two kingdoms following Solomon's death.

And he said to Jeroboam, "Take for yourself ten pieces, for thus says the Lord, the God of Israel: 'Behold, I will tear the kingdom out of the hand of Solomon and will give ten tribes to you but he shall have one tribe for the sake of My servant David, and for the sake of Jerusalem, the city which I have chosen out of all the tribes of Israel'" (1 Kings 11:31-32).

3. All that Solomon built was captured or destroyed by the enemies of God.

And in the fifth month, on the seventh day of the month (which was the nineteenth year of King Nebuchadnezzar king of Babylon), Nebuzaradan the captain of the guard, a servant of the king of Babylon, came to Jerusalem. He burned the house of the Lord and the king's house; all the houses of Jerusalem, that is, all the houses of the great, he burned with fire. And all the army of the Chaldeans who were with the captain of the guard broke down the walls of Jerusalem all around (2 Kings 25:8-10).

I. **Why and How Did God Allow the Nation of Israel to Be Destroyed?**

    1.   God destroyed Israel because they did not walk in faith and obedience to Him. They chose to serve the false gods of the nations around them.

And they rejected His statutes and His covenant that He had made with their fathers, and His testimonies which He had testified against them; they followed idols, became idolaters, and went after the nations who were all around them, concerning whom the Lord had charged them that they should not do like them. So they left all the commandments of the Lord their God, made for themselves a molded image and two calves, made a wooden image and worshiped all the host of heaven, and served Baal. And they caused their sons and daughters to pass through the fire, practiced witchcraft and soothsaying, and sold themselves to do evil in the sight of the Lord, to provoke Him to anger (2 Kings 17:15-17).

    2.   God destroyed even the remnant tribe of Judah for her unfaithfulness.

But they paid no attention, and Manasseh seduced them to do more evil than the nations whom the

Establishing the Kingdom

Lord had destroyed before the children of Israel. And the Lord spoke by His servants the prophets, saying, "Because Manasseh king of Judah has done these abominations (he has acted more wickedly than all the Amorites who were before him, and has also made Judah sin with his idols), therefore thus says the Lord God of Israel: 'Behold, I am bringing such calamity upon Jerusalem and Judah, that whoever hears of it, both his ears will tingle'" (2 Kings 21:9-12).

3. After warning the northern tribes of Israel by faithful prophets, God allowed them to be carried into captivity by Assyria.

And the Lord rejected all the descendants of Israel, afflicted them, and delivered them into the hand of plunderers, until He had cast them from His sight (2 Kings 17:20).

4. After warning the southern tribes in the nation of Judah, the Lord allowed them to be carried away into captivity in Babylon for 70 years.

And the Lord said, "I will also remove Judah from My sight, as I have removed Israel, and will cast off this city Jerusalem which I have chosen, and the house of which I said, 'My name shall be there'" (2 Kings 23:27).

And this whole land shall be a desolation and an astonishment, and these nations shall serve the king of Babylon seventy years (Jeremiah 25:11).

From Covenant to Kingdom

J. How Did the Issues of Faith and Obedience Enter Into the Fate of Israel?

The kings that followed David in Judah were not always as faithful and obedient to the Lord as he was.

Ahaz was twenty years old when he became king, and he reigned sixteen years in Jerusalem; and he did not do what was right in the sight of the Lord his God, as his father David had done (2 Kings 16:2).

And he did what was right in the sight of the Lord, and walked in all the ways of his father David; he did not turn aside to the right hand or to the left (2 Kings 22:2).

Let's Review What We Have Learned About the Kings of Israel.

1. The Lord Himself was to be _____ over Israel. It is the Lord who is King over all those who have submitted themselves to His reign.

Establishing the Kingdom

2. The nation of Israel rejected God as King over them and God gave them a king like the nations around them had. What was this king's name? _____

3. Saul later failed to _____ obey the word of the Lord through Samuel the prophet. The _____ as well as the _____ was taken from him.

4. David was "a man after God's own heart." David was a man of _____ and _____ to the Lord.

5. It was through David's reign that God prophetically revealed His spiritual purpose in Christ _____ and in the _____. *David* is a prophetic name for Christ.

6. Solomon was charged by God to build Him a great _____, a place where God's _____ would dwell on earth.

7. Solomon failed God by taking wives from heathen nations and allowing them to bring their _____.

Dig a Little Deeper; Grow a Little Closer

1. Read all of First Samuel 15 and especially the key verse that is printed below.

Then Samuel said: "Has the Lord as great delight in burnt offerings and sacrifices, as in obeying the voice of the Lord? Behold, to obey is better than sacrifice, and to heed than the fat of rams" (1 Samuel 15:22).

2. As you read these verses, what was the instruction that God gave to Saul through Samuel? How did Saul not fully obey the Lord's instructions?

From Covenant to Kingdom

_____
_____
_____

3. What is God telling us about obedience in verse 22? The sacrifices represent religious activity. What is the Scripture telling us about religion and relationship?

_____
_____
_____

4. Are there areas in your life where you are just going through the motions of religion and not fully obeying the Lord? List any areas of concern here.

_____
_____
_____

Establishing the Kingdom

Review Notes

III. The Message of the Prophets

A. What Is a Prophet?

1. A prophet is one who speaks the word of God to His people under the inspiration of the Holy Spirit.

Formerly in Israel, when a man went to inquire of God, he spoke thus: "Come, let us go to the seer"; for he who is now called a prophet was formerly called a seer (1 Samuel 9:9).

2. A prophet calls the people of God to faith and obedience in the Lord.

And it shall come to pass in that day that the remnant of Israel, and such as have escaped of the house of Jacob, will never again depend on him who defeated them, but will depend on the Lord, the Holy One of Israel, in truth (Isaiah 10:20).

For thus says the Lord God, the Holy One of Israel: "In returning and rest you shall be saved; in quietness and confidence shall be your strength..." (Isaiah 30:15).

When you cry out, let your collection of idols deliver you. But the wind will carry them all away, a breath will take them. But he who puts his trust in Me shall possess the land, and shall inherit My holy mountain (Isaiah 57:13).

3. A prophet may speak of what is going to happen in the future.

I was watching in the night visions, and behold, One like the Son of Man, coming with the clouds of

The Message of the Prophets

heaven! He came to the Ancient of Days, and they brought Him near before Him. Then to Him was given dominion and glory and a kingdom, that all peoples, nations, and languages should serve Him. His dominion is an everlasting dominion, which shall not pass away, and His kingdom the one which shall not be destroyed (Daniel 7:13-14).

4. A prophet sometimes prophesies with musical accompaniment.

"But now bring me a musician." Then it happened, when the musician played, that the hand of the Lord came upon him (2 Kings 3:15).

B. Who Were the Prophets of the Old Testament?

1. There was the group we call the Major Prophets:

Isaiah	Ezekiel
Jeremiah	Daniel

2. There was the group we call the Minor Prophets. (They were not called minor because of the level of importance of the messages they spoke.)

Hosea	Obadiah	Nahum	Haggai
Joel	Jonah	Habakkuk	Zechariah
Amos	Micah	Zephaniah	Malachi

C. What Rules Must We Follow in Order to Understand the Words of the Prophets?

1. To understand the prophets we must remember that the Bible is a spiritual book. We must have the Holy Spirit's help to understand them.

Knowing this first, that no prophecy of Scripture is of any private interpretation, for prophecy never came by the will of man, but holy men of God spoke as they were moved by the Holy Spirit (2 Peter 1:20-21).

Then the Spirit of the Lord fell upon me, and said to me, "Speak! Thus says the Lord: 'Thus you have said, O house of Israel; for I know the things that come into your mind'" (Ezekiel 11:5).

2. To understand the prophets we must read them in light of the times in which they were written. This is called historical context.

3. To understand the prophets we must read them in terms of fulfillment in the New Testament.

The Message of the Prophets

But Peter, standing up with the eleven, raised his voice and said to them, "Men of Judea and all who dwell in Jerusalem, let this be known to you, and heed my words...But this is what was spoken by the prophet Joel" (Acts 2:14,16).

Then He closed the book, and gave it back to the attendant and sat down. And the eyes of all who were in the synagogue were fixed on Him. And He began to say to them, "Today this Scripture is fulfilled in your hearing" (Luke 4:20-21).

And in them the prophecy of Isaiah is fulfilled, which says: "Hearing you will hear and shall not understand, and seeing you will see and not perceive; For the hearts of this people have grown dull. Their ears are hard of hearing, and their eyes they have closed, lest they should see with their eyes and hear with their ears, lest they should understand with their hearts and turn, so that I should heal them." But blessed are your eyes for they see, and your ears for they hear; for assuredly, I say to you that many prophets and righteous men desired to see what you see, and did not see it, and to hear what you hear, and did not hear it (Matthew 13:14-17).

4. To understand the prophets we must read them in light of their future fulfillment.

Repent therefore and be converted, that your sins may be blotted out, so that times of refreshing may come from the presence of the Lord, and that He may send Jesus Christ, who was preached to you before, whom heaven must receive until the times of restoration of all things, which God has spoken by the mouth of all His holy prophets since the world began (Acts 3:19-21).

D. What Was the Mission of the Prophets?

1. The mission of the prophets was to call the nations of Israel and Judah back to faith and obedience to God.

Seek the Lord while He may be found, call upon Him while He is near. Let the wicked forsake his way, and the unrighteous man his thoughts; let him return to the Lord, and He will have mercy on him; and to our God, for He will abundantly pardon (Isaiah 55:6-7).

And the Lord has sent to you all His servants the prophets, rising early and sending them, but you have not listened nor inclined your ear to hear. They said, "Repent now everyone of his evil way and his evil doings, and dwell in the land that the Lord has given to you and your fathers forever and ever. Do not go after other gods to serve them and worship them, and do not provoke Me to anger with the works of your hands; and I will not harm you" (Jeremiah 25:4-6).

2. The mission of the prophets was to remind the people of the covenant between the nation and their God.

Yet the Lord testified against Israel and against Judah, by all of His prophets, every seer, saying, "Turn from your evil ways, and keep My commandments and My statutes, according to all the law which I commanded your fathers, and which I sent to you by My servants the prophets" (2 Kings 17:13).

I have also sent to you all My servants the prophets, rising up early and sending them, saying, "Turn now everyone from his evil way, amend your doings, and do not go after other gods to serve them; then you will dwell in the land which I have given you and your fathers." But you have not inclined your ear, nor obeyed Me (Jeremiah 35:15).

E.   What Was the Message of the Prophets?

1. The message of the prophets to Israel and Judah was that they must turn from their evil ways and back to God.

Yet the Lord testified against Israel and against Judah, by all of His prophets, every seer, saying, "Turn from your evil ways, and keep My commandments and My statutes, according to all the law which I commanded your fathers, and which I sent to you by My servants the prophets" (2 Kings 17:13).

Seek the Lord while He may be found, call upon Him while He is near. Let the wicked forsake his way, and the unrighteous man his thoughts; let him return to the Lord, and He will have mercy on him; and to our God, for He will abundantly pardon (Isaiah 55:6-7).

2. The message of the prophets was that judgment would come upon those who did not repent.

Now the end has come upon you, and I will send My anger against you; I will judge you according to your ways, and I will repay you for all your abominations. My eye will not spare you, nor will I have pity; but I will repay your ways, and your abominations will be in your midst; then you shall know that I am the Lord! (Ezekiel 7:3-4)

"Therefore I will judge you, O house of Israel, every one according to his ways," says the Lord God. "Repent, and turn from all your transgressions, so that iniquity will not be your ruin. Cast away from you all the transgressions which you have committed, and get yourselves a new heart and a new spirit. For why should you die, O house of Israel? For I have no pleasure in the death of one who dies," says the Lord God. "Therefore turn and live!" (Ezekiel 18:30-32)

3. The message of the prophets was that a remnant would survive the captivity.

And it shall come to pass in that day that the remnant of Israel, and such as have escaped of the house of Jacob, will never again depend on him who defeated them, but will depend on the Lord, the Holy One of Israel, in truth. The remnant will return, the remnant of Jacob, to the Mighty God (Isaiah 10:20-21).

But I will gather the remnant of My flock out of all countries where I have driven them, and bring them back to their folds; and they shall be fruitful and increase (Jeremiah 23:3).

The Message of the Prophets

F. What Did the Prophets Say Concerning Jesus Christ?

1. The prophets said that out of the remnant would come the Savior of the world from the line of David.

There shall come forth a Rod from the stem of Jesse, and a Branch shall grow out of his roots (Isaiah 11:1).

"Behold, the days are coming," says the Lord, "that I will raise to David a Branch of righteousness; a King shall reign and prosper, and execute judgment and righteousness in the earth. In His days Judah will be saved, and Israel will dwell safely; now this is His name by which He will be called: THE LORD OUR RIGHTEOUSNESS" (Jeremiah 23:5-6).

In those days and at that time I will cause to grow up to David a Branch of righteousness; he shall execute judgment and righteousness in the earth (Jeremiah 33:15).

2. This Savior would suffer and die to save His people from sin.

Surely He has borne our griefs and carried our sorrows; yet we esteemed Him stricken, smitten by God, and afflicted. But He was wounded for our transgressions, he was bruised for our iniquities; the chastisement for our peace was upon Him, and by His stripes we are healed. All we like sheep have gone astray; we have turned, every one, to his own way; and the Lord has laid on Him the iniquity of us all. He was oppressed and He was afflicted, yet He opened not His mouth; he was led as a lamb to the slaughter, and as a sheep before its shearers is silent, so He opened not His mouth (Isaiah 53:4-7).

3. This Savior would bring them into a New Covenant that would include all people, Jews and Gentiles alike.

Arise, shine; for your light has come! And the glory of the Lord is risen upon you. For behold, the darkness shall cover the earth, and deep darkness the people; but the Lord will arise over you, and His glory will be seen upon you. The Gentiles shall come to your light, and kings to the brightness of your rising. Lift up your eyes all around, and see: they all gather together, they come to you; your sons shall come from afar, and your daughters shall be nursed at your side (Isaiah 60:1-4).

"Behold, the days are coming," says the Lord, "when I will make a new covenant with the house of Israel and with the house of Judah—not according to the covenant that I made with their fathers in the day that I took them by the hand to lead them out of the land of Egypt, My covenant which they broke, though I was a husband to them," says the Lord. "But this is the covenant that I will make with the house of Israel after those days," says the Lord: "I will put My law in their minds, and write it on their hearts; and I will be their God, and they shall be My people. No more shall every man teach his neighbor, and every man his brother, saying, 'Know the Lord,' for they all shall know Me, from the least of them to the greatest of them," says the

The Message of the Prophets

Lord. "For I will forgive their iniquity, and their sin I will remember no more." Thus says the Lord, who gives the sun for a light by day, the ordinances of the moon and the stars for a light by night, who disturbs the sea, and its waves roar (the Lord of hosts is His name) (Jeremiah 31:31-35).

For this is My blood of the new covenant, which is shed for many for the remission of sins (Matthew 26:28).

4. This Savior would establish an everlasting kingdom.

And in the days of these kings the God of heaven will set up a kingdom which shall never be destroyed; and the kingdom shall not be left to other people; it shall break in pieces and consume all these kingdoms, and it shall stand forever (Daniel 2:44).

Then they shall dwell in the land that I have given to Jacob My servant, where your fathers dwelt; and they shall dwell there, they, their children, and their children's children, forever; and My servant David shall be their prince forever (Ezekiel 37:25).

G. **What Was the Message of the Prophets Concerning the Church?**

1. The prophets said that God would pour out His Spirit on those in the New Covenant.

For I will pour water on him who is thirsty, and floods on the dry ground; I will pour My Spirit on your descendants, and My blessing on your offspring; They will spring up among the grass like willows by the watercourses (Isaiah 44:3-4).

For the Lord will comfort Zion, He will comfort all her waste places; He will make her wilderness like Eden, and her desert like the garden of the Lord; joy and gladness will be found in it, thanksgiving and the voice of melody (Isaiah 51:3).

To console those who mourn in Zion, to give them beauty for ashes, the oil of joy for mourning, the garment of praise for the spirit of heaviness; that they may be called trees of righteousness, the planting of the Lord, that He may be glorified. And they shall rebuild the old ruins, they shall raise up the former desolations, and they shall repair the ruined cities, the desolations of many generations (Isaiah 61:3-4).

And it shall come to pass afterward that I will pour out My Spirit on all flesh; your sons and your daughters shall prophesy, your old men shall dream dreams, your young men shall see visions (Joel 2:28).

2. The prophets said that God would rebuild the tabernacle of David through the Church. The reign of Christ from the house (tabernacle) of David would continue for all people—not just the nation of Israel.

On that day I will raise up the tabernacle of David, which has fallen down, and repair its damages; I will raise up its ruins, and rebuild it as in the days of old (Amos 9:11).

The Message of the Prophets

In mercy the throne will be established; and One will sit on it in truth, in the tabernacle of David, judging and seeking justice and hastening righteousness (Isaiah 16:5).

"After this I will return and will rebuild the tabernacle of David, which has fallen down; I will rebuild its ruins, and I will set it up; so that the rest of mankind may seek the Lord, even all the Gentiles who are called by My name," says the Lord who does all these things (Acts 15:16-17).

3. The prophets said that the Church would minister in the power and anointing of the Holy Spirit to restore those saved from sin and captivity.

The Spirit of the Lord God is upon Me, because the Lord has anointed Me to preach good tidings to the poor; He has sent Me to heal the brokenhearted, to proclaim liberty to the captives, and the opening of the prison to those who are bound; to proclaim the acceptable year of the Lord, and the day of vengeance of our God; to comfort all who mourn, to console those who mourn in Zion, to give them beauty for ashes, the oil of joy for mourning, the garment of praise for the spirit of heaviness; that they may be called trees of righteousness, the planting of the Lord, that He may be glorified. And they shall rebuild the old ruins, they shall raise up the former desolations, and they shall repair the ruined cities, the desolations of many generations (Isaiah 61:1-4).

4. The prophets said that the Church would have dominion over evil.

Arise and thresh, O daughter of Zion; for I will make your horn iron, and I will make your hooves bronze; you shall beat in pieces many peoples; I will consecrate their gain to the Lord, and their substance to the Lord of the whole earth (Micah 4:13).

"Indeed they shall surely assemble, but not because of Me. Whoever assembles against you shall fall for your sake...No weapon formed against you shall prosper, and every tongue which rises against you in judgment you shall condemn. This is the heritage of the servants of the Lord, and their righteousness is from Me," says the Lord (Isaiah 54:15,17).

5. The prophets said that the Church would be a purified and righteous people.

But you shall be named the priests of the Lord, they shall call you the servants of our God. You shall eat the riches of the Gentiles, and in their glory you shall boast (Isaiah 61:6).

He will sit as a refiner and a purifier of silver; he will purify the sons of Levi, and purge them as gold and silver, that they may offer to the Lord an offering in righteousness. Then the offering of Judah and Jerusalem will be pleasant to the Lord, as in the days of old, as in former years (Malachi 3:3-4).

A highway shall be there, and a road, and it shall be called the Highway of Holiness. The unclean

The Message of the Prophets

shall not pass over it, but it shall be for others. Whoever walks the road, although a fool, shall not go astray. No lion shall be there, nor shall any ravenous beast go up on it; it shall not be found there. But the redeemed shall walk there (Isaiah 35:8-9).

6. The prophets said that through the Church, the earth would be filled with the knowledge of the glory of the Lord.

For the earth will be filled with the knowledge of the glory of the Lord, as the waters cover the sea (Habakkuk 2:14).

They shall not hurt nor destroy in all My holy mountain, for the earth shall be full of the knowledge of the Lord as the waters cover the sea (Isaiah 11:9).

And in that day it shall be that living waters shall flow from Jerusalem, half of them toward the eastern sea and half of them toward the western sea; in both summer and winter it shall occur. And the Lord shall be King over all the earth. In that day it shall be—"The Lord is one," and His name one (Zechariah 14:8-9).

7. The prophets said that Jesus Christ would return for His glorious and spotless Bride, the Church.

I was watching in the night visions, and behold, One like the Son of Man, coming with the clouds of heaven! He came to the Ancient of Days, and they brought Him near before Him. Then to Him was given dominion and glory and a kingdom, that all peoples, nations, and languages should serve Him. His dominion is an everlasting dominion, which shall not pass away, and His kingdom the one which shall not be destroyed (Daniel 7:13-14).

You shall also be a crown of glory in the hand of the Lord, and a royal diadem in the hand of your God. You shall no longer be termed Forsaken, nor shall your land any more be termed Desolate; but you shall be called Hephzibah, and your land Beulah; for the Lord delights in you, and your land shall be married. For as a young man marries a virgin, so shall your sons marry you; and as the bridegroom rejoices over the bride, so shall your God rejoice over you (Isaiah 62:3-5).

8. The prophets said that worship would be restored in the Church.

"The voice of joy and the voice of gladness, the voice of the bridegroom and the voice of the bride, the voice of those who will say: 'Praise the Lord of hosts, for the Lord is good, for His mercy endures forever' and of those who will bring the sacrifice of praise into the house of the Lord. For I will cause the captives of the land to return as at the first," says the Lord (Jeremiah 33:11).

Let's Review What We Have Learned About the Prophets.

1. A prophet is one who speaks the _____ of God to His people under the inspiration of the _____ .

The Message of the Prophets

2. A prophet calls the people of God to _____ and _____ in the Lord.

3. Name at least two of the Major Prophets of the Old Testament.

_____

_____

_____

_____

4. Name at least four of the Minor Prophets.

_____

_____

_____

_____

5. The message of the prophets was that _____ would come upon those who did not _____.

6. The prophets said that out of the remnant would come the _____ of the world from the line of _____.

7. This Savior would establish an _____ kingdom.

8. The prophets said that the Church would minister in the _____ and _____ of the Holy Spirit to restore those saved from sin and captivity.

Dig a Little Deeper; Grow a Little Closer

If you are willing and obedient, you shall eat the good of the land (Isaiah 1:19).

From Covenant to Kingdom

Therefore the Lord said: "Inasmuch as these people draw near with their mouths and honor Me with their lips, but have removed their hearts far from Me, and their fear toward Me is taught by the commandment of men" (Isaiah 29:13).

1. The verses printed above give us the essence of the prophetic mission, which was to call people back to faith and obedience in the Lord. As you read these verses, what are the two things that are necessary to eat the good of the land?

_____

_____

_____

_____

2. What do you think "eat the good of the land" means?

_____

_____

_____

_____

3. According to this verse it is possible to be obedient but not willing. In other words, "I'll do what you say but not from my heart." Isaiah says that people have removed their hearts from God. Are there places in your life where you are obedient but your heart is not really in it—places where you give the Lord lip service and not full devotion? List those places here and give them to the Lord in prayer.

The Message of the Prophets

From Covenant to Kingdom

Review Notes

IV. Restoring the Remnant of Israel

A. For What Purpose Did God Preserve a Remnant of Israel?

1. God always preserves a "remnant," a holy seed through which to continue His purposes and carry out His word.

Unless the Lord of hosts had left to us a very small remnant, we would have become like Sodom, we would have been made like Gomorrah (Isaiah 1:9).

The Lord has removed men far away, and the forsaken places are many in the midst of the land. But yet a tenth will be in it, and will return and be for consuming, as a terebinth tree or as an oak, whose stump remains when it is cut down. So the holy seed shall be its stump (Isaiah 6:12-13).

For though your people, O Israel, be as the sand of the sea, a remnant of them will return; the destruction decreed shall overflow with righteousness (Isaiah 10:22).

2. God preserved the remnant to prepare the way for Jesus Christ to be born.

There shall come forth a Rod from the stem of Jesse, and a Branch shall grow out of his roots (Isaiah 11:1).

And your house and your kingdom shall be established forever before you. Your throne shall be established forever (2 Samuel 7:16).

These twelve Jesus sent out and commanded them, saying: "Do not go into the way of the Gentiles, and do not enter a city of the Samaritans. But go rather to the lost sheep of the house of Israel" (Matthew 10:5-6).

Who are Israelites, to whom pertain the adoption, the glory, the covenants, the giving of the law, the service of God, and the promises; of whom are the fathers and from whom, according to the flesh, Christ came, who is over all, the eternally blessed God. Amen (Romans 9:4-5).

3. God preserved a remnant to restore Jerusalem.

And they said to me, "The survivors who are left from the captivity in the province are there in great distress and reproach. The wall of Jerusalem is also broken down, and its gates are burned with fire" (Nehemiah 1:3).

And I said to the king, "If it pleases the king, and if your servant has found favor in your sight, I ask that you send me to Judah, to the city of my fathers' tombs, that I may rebuild it" (Nehemiah 2:5).

4. God preserved a remnant to restore His house.

Thus says Cyrus king of Persia: All the kingdoms of the earth the Lord God of heaven has given me. And He has commanded me to build Him a house at Jerusalem which is in Judah. Who is among you of all His people? May his God be with him, and let him go up to Jerusalem which is in Judah, and build the house of the Lord God of Israel (He is God), which is in Jerusalem (Ezra 1:2-3).

5. God preserved the remnant to restore His law.

Now all the people gathered together as one man in the open square that was in front of the Water Gate; and they told Ezra the scribe to bring the Book of the Law of Moses, which the Lord had commanded Israel...Then he read from it in the open square that was in front of the Water Gate from morning until midday, before the men and women and those who could understand; and the ears of all the people were attentive to the Book of the Law...So they read distinctly from the book, in the Law of God; and they gave the sense, and helped them to understand the reading (Nehemiah 8:1,3,8).

B. **How Did God Preserve the Remnant of Israel?**

1. God called the remnant to return from their captivity back to Israel in fulfillment of His word through the prophets.

For thus says the Lord: After seventy years are completed at Babylon, I will visit you and perform My good word toward you, and cause you to return to this place (Jeremiah 29:10).

In the first year of his reign I, Daniel, understood by the books the number of the years specified by the word of the Lord through Jeremiah the prophet, that He would accomplish seventy years in the desolations of Jerusalem (Daniel 9:2).

2. God chose Cyrus, the king of Persia, to destroy Babylon and to allow the Jews to return to Israel following 70 years (606 B.C. to 536 B.C.) of captivity.

Who says of Cyrus, "He is My shepherd, and he shall perform all My pleasure, saying to Jerusalem, 'You shall be built,' and to the temple, 'Your foundation shall be laid'" (Isaiah 44:28).

Thus says the Lord to His anointed, to Cyrus, whose right hand I have held—to subdue nations before him and loose the armor of kings, to open before him the double doors, so that the gates will not be shut…"I will give you the treasures of darkness and hidden riches of secret places, that you may know that I, the Lord, who call you by your name, am the God of Israel. For Jacob My servant's sake, and Israel My elect, I have even called you by your name; I have named you, though you have not known Me" (Isaiah 45:1,3-4).

Now in the first year of Cyrus king of Persia, that the word of the Lord by the mouth of Jeremiah might be fulfilled, the Lord stirred up the spirit of Cyrus king of Persia, so that he made a proclamation throughout all his kingdom, and also put it in writing, saying, Thus says Cyrus king of Persia: All the kingdoms of the earth the Lord God of heaven has given me. And He has commanded me to build Him a house at Jerusalem which is in Judah. Who is among you of all His people? May his God be with him, and let him go up to Jerusalem which is in Judah, and build the house of the Lord God of Israel (He is God), which is in Jerusalem. And whoever is left in any place where he dwells, let the men of his place help him with silver and gold, with goods and livestock, besides the freewill offerings for the house of God which is in Jerusalem (Ezra 1:1-4).

C. **Who Did God Choose to Lead This Remnant? What Were Their Roles?**

    1.   Zerubbabel was the governor when the temple was rebuilt in 536-516 B.C. He was also a direct descendant of King David, through whom Jesus Christ would be born. He represents Jesus Christ, who would build His Church.

The hands of Zerubbabel have laid the foundation of this temple; his hands shall also finish it. Then you will know that the Lord of hosts has sent Me to you (Zechariah 4:9).

And after they were brought to Babylon, Jeconiah begot Shealtiel, and Shealtiel begot Zerubbabel. Zerubbabel begot Abiud, Abiud begot Eliakim, and Eliakim begot Azor. Azor begot Zadok, Zadok begot Achim, and Achim begot Eliud. Eliud begot Eleazar, Eleazar begot Matthan, and Matthan begot Jacob. And Jacob begot Joseph the husband of Mary, of whom was born Jesus who is called Christ (Matthew 1:12-16).

    2.   Joshua was the high priest during the time of Zerubbabel.

So Zerubbabel the son of Shealtiel and Jeshua the son of Jozadak rose up and began to build the house of God which is in Jerusalem; and the prophets of God were with them, helping them (Ezra 5:2).

Take the silver and gold, make an elaborate crown, and set it on the head of Joshua the son of Jehozadak, the high priest. Then speak to him, saying, "Thus says the Lord of hosts, saying: 'Behold, the Man whose name is the BRANCH! From His place He shall branch out, and He shall build the temple of the Lord; Yes, He shall build the temple of the Lord. He shall bear the glory, and shall sit and rule on His throne; so He shall be a priest on His throne, and the counsel of peace shall be between them both'" (Zechariah 6:11-13).

3. Haggai was responsible for re-starting the building of the temple after it was stopped out of fear for 15 years. He prophetically saw the glory of the Church, God's ultimate temple.

Then the prophet Haggai and Zechariah the son of Iddo, prophets, prophesied to the Jews who were in Judah and Jerusalem, in the name of the God of Israel, who was over them. So Zerubbabel the son of Shealtiel and Jeshua the son of Jozadak rose up and began to build the house of God which is in Jerusalem; and the prophets of God were with them, helping them (Ezra 5:1-2).

"The glory of this latter temple shall be greater than the former," says the Lord of hosts. "And in

Restoring the Remnant of Israel

this place I will give peace," says the Lord of hosts (Haggai 2:9).

4. Zechariah was another prophet who encouraged the rebuilding of the temple. He had a revelation of righteousness being restored through Christ.

Then the prophet Haggai and Zechariah the son of Iddo, prophets, prophesied to the Jews who were in Judah and Jerusalem, in the name of the God of Israel, who was over them. So Zerubbabel the son of Shealtiel and Jeshua the son of Jozadak rose up and began to build the house of God which is in Jerusalem; and the prophets of God were with them, helping them (Ezra 5:1-2).

In that day a fountain shall be opened for the house of David and for the inhabitants of Jerusalem, for sin and for uncleanness (Zechariah 13:1).

5. Ezra was a priestly scribe who returned to Jerusalem with Zerubbabel. He was a key figure during the time of Nehemiah in restoring the law to the returning remnant of Israel.

Now these are the priests and the Levites who came up with Zerubbabel the son of Shealtiel, and Jeshua: Seraiah, Jeremiah, Ezra (Nehemiah 12:1).

6. Nehemiah was a trusted servant (cupbearer) to the king of Persia. He was allowed by the king to return to Jerusalem to complete

the rebuilding of that city by repairing the gates and walls.

D. What Was the Opposition That the Returning Remnant Faced As They Rebuilt Jerusalem?

1. The remnant faced satanic opposition.

Now it happened, when Sanballat, Tobiah, the Arabs, the Ammonites, and the Ashdodites heard that the walls of Jerusalem were being restored and the gaps were beginning to be closed, that they became very angry, and all of them conspired together to come and attack Jerusalem and create confusion. Nevertheless we made our prayer to our God, and because of them we set a watch against them day and night (Nehemiah 4:7-9).

2. The remnant faced opposition within the walls of Jerusalem:

From the debris of old ideas and dead works:

Then Judah said, "The strength of the laborers is failing, and there is so much rubbish that we are not able to build the wall" (Nehemiah 4:10).

From the fear of the enemy:

And our adversaries said, "They will neither know nor see anything, till we come into their midst and kill them and cause the work to cease." So it was, when the Jews who dwelt near them came, that they told us ten times, "From whatever place you turn, they will be upon us" (Nehemiah 4:11-12).

And from the temptation of self-gain.

After serious thought, I rebuked the nobles and rulers, and said to them, "Each of you is exacting usury from his brother." So I called a great assembly against them. And I said to them, "According to our ability we have redeemed our Jewish brethren who were sold to the nations. Now indeed, will you even sell your brethren? Or should they be sold to us?" Then they were silenced and found nothing to say (Nehemiah 5:7-8).

3. The remnant faced opposition outside the walls of Jerusalem:

From the scorn and ridicule of the enemies of God's purpose:

But it so happened, when Sanballat heard that we were rebuilding the wall, that he was furious and very indignant, and mocked the Jews. And he spoke before his brethren and the army of Samaria, and said, "What are these feeble Jews doing? Will they fortify themselves? Will they offer sacrifices? Will they complete it in a day? Will they revive the stones from the heaps of rubbish—stones that are burned?" Now Tobiah the Ammonite was beside him, and he said, "Whatever they build, if even a fox goes up on it, he will break down their stone wall" (Nehemiah 4:1-3).

From delaying tactics and threats of war by neighbors:

Then the people of the land tried to discourage the people of Judah. They troubled them in building, and hired counselors against them to frustrate their purpose all the days of Cyrus king of Persia, even until the reign of Darius king of Persia (Ezra 4:4-5).

Now it happened, when Sanballat, Tobiah, the Arabs, the Ammonites, and the Ashdodites heard that the walls of Jerusalem were being restored and the gaps were beginning to be closed, that they became very angry, and all of them conspired together to come and attack Jerusalem and create confusion (Nehemiah 4:7-8).

And you have also appointed prophets to proclaim concerning you at Jerusalem, saying, "There is a king in Judah!" Now these matters will be reported to the king. So come, therefore, and let us consult together (Nehemiah 6:7).

And from the stealth and lies of those who sought to stop the work of God.

Sanballat and Geshem sent to me, saying, "Come, let us meet together among the villages in the plain of Ono." But they thought to do me harm. So I sent messengers to them, saying, "I am doing a great work, so that I cannot come down. Why should the work cease while I leave it and go down to you?" (Nehemiah 6:2-3)

E. What Lessons Can Be Learned From the Return of the Remnant?

1. We learn that we must continue to do the will and work of God despite opposition.

I am doing a great work, so that I cannot come down. Why should the work cease while I leave it and go down to you? (Nehemiah 6:2-3)

2. We learn that we can only work effectively when our hearts are devoted to the work

and the leaders that God has placed ahead of us.

And when the seventh month had come, and the children of Israel were in the cities, the people gathered together as one man to Jerusalem (Ezra 3:1).

So we built the wall, and the entire wall was joined together up to half its height, for the people had a mind to work (Nehemiah 4:6).

3. We learn that it is God who is worthy of our praise when we do His work.

And they sang responsively, praising and giving thanks to the Lord: "For He is good, for His mercy endures forever toward Israel." Then all the people shouted with a great shout, when they praised the Lord, because the foundation of the house of the Lord was laid (Ezra 3:11).

And the heads of the Levites were Hashabiah, Sherebiah, and Jeshua the son of Kadmiel, with their brothers across from them, to praise and give thanks, group alternating with group, according to the command of David the man of God (Nehemiah 12:24).

4. We learn that God sends His word ahead of His work through the prophets.

So the elders of the Jews built, and they prospered through the prophesying of Haggai the prophet and Zechariah the son of Iddo. And they built and finished it, according to the commandment of the God of Israel, and according to the command of

Cyrus, Darius, and Artaxerxes king of Persia (Ezra 6:14).

So the Lord stirred up the spirit of Zerubbabel the son of Shealtiel, governor of Judah, and the spirit of Joshua the son of Jehozadak, the high priest, and the spirit of all the remnant of the people; and they came and worked on the house of the Lord of hosts, their God (Haggai 1:14).

F. What Meaning Does the Restoration of the Remnant Hold for Us Today?

1. The restoration of the temple points to Jesus Christ building His Church out of living stones.

"The glory of this latter temple shall be greater than the former," says the Lord of hosts. "And in this place I will give peace," says the Lord of hosts (Haggai 2:9).

Restoring the Remnant of Israel

Now, therefore, you are no longer strangers and foreigners, but fellow citizens with the saints and members of the household of God, having been built on the foundation of the apostles and prophets, Jesus Christ Himself being the chief corner stone, in whom the whole building, being joined together, grows into a holy temple in the Lord, in whom you also are being built together for a dwelling place of God in the Spirit (Ephesians 2:19-22).

You also, as living stones, are being built up a spiritual house, a holy priesthood, to offer up spiritual sacrifices acceptable to God through Jesus Christ (1 Peter 2:5).

2. The restoration of the wall points to the security that we now have in Christ Jesus through repentance, baptism, and the infilling of the Holy Spirit.

Then Peter said to them, "Repent, and let every one of you be baptized in the name of Jesus Christ for the remission of sins; and you shall receive the gift of the Holy Spirit" (Acts 2:38).

He has delivered us from the power of darkness and conveyed us into the kingdom of the Son of His love (Colossians 1:13).

And He said to me, "My grace is sufficient for you, for My strength is made perfect in weakness." Therefore most gladly I will rather boast in my infirmities, that the power of Christ may rest upon me (2 Corinthians 12:9).

3. The restoration of the law points to the eternal nature of the law that is now written on the hearts of those in the new covenant through Jesus Christ.

And it is easier for heaven and earth to pass away than for one tittle of the law to fail (Luke 16:17).

For the law of the Spirit of life in Christ Jesus has made me free from the law of sin and death. For what the law could not do in that it was weak through the flesh, God did by sending His own Son in the likeness of sinful flesh, on account of sin: He condemned sin in the flesh (Romans 8:2-3).

Let's Review What We Have Learned About the Remnant of Israel.

1. God always preserves a "remnant," a _____ through which to continue His _____ and carry out His word.

2. List the three things that the remnant was to restore.

_____

_____

_____

3. List three sources of opposition to the work of restoration.

_____

_____

_____

Restoring the Remnant of Israel

4. _____ prophetically saw the glory of the Church, God's ultimate temple.

5. _____ was a key figure in restoring the law to the remnant of Israel.

6. _____ was a trusted servant of the king of Persia who returned to rebuild the walls and gates of Jerusalem.

7. The restoration of the temple points to Jesus Christ building His _____ out of _____.

8. We learn that God sends His _____ ahead of His work through the _____.

Dig a Little Deeper; Grow a Little Closer

1. Read the following passage from the Book of Nehemiah.

But it so happened, when Sanballat heard that we were rebuilding the wall, that he was furious and very indignant, and mocked the Jews. And he spoke before his brethren and the army of Samaria, and said, "What are these feeble Jews doing? Will they fortify themselves? Will they offer sacrifices? Will they complete it in a day? Will they revive the stones from the heaps of rubbish—stones that are burned?" Now Tobiah the Ammonite was beside him, and he said, "Whatever they build, if even a fox goes up on it, he will break down their stone wall." Hear, O our God, for we are despised; turn their reproach on their own heads, and give them as plunder to a land of captivity! Do not cover their iniquity, and do not let their sin be blotted out from before You; for they have provoked You to anger before the builders. So we built the wall, and the entire wall was joined together up to half its height, for the people had a mind to work (Nehemiah 4:1-6).

2. Sanballat is a representation of satan, the enemy of God's purposes. What was the reaction of Sanballat to the rebuilding of the walls?

_____

_____

_____

_____

3. Have you ever experienced any of the things that Nehemiah did as God was doing a work in or through your life? What was it?

_____

_____

_____

_____

4. How did Nehemiah respond to the ridicule and doubt cast by the enemies of God's purpose? How should you respond when you encounter opposition to the Lord's ongoing works in your life?

_____

_____

_____

_____

— # Review Notes

From Covenant to Kingdom

Be sure to enter into the journal in this book how God responds to what you have prayed.

Books in the *Laying the FOUNDATION* Series:

Book 1—The Nature of God
- I. The Nature of God
- II. The Bible
- III. The Creation

Book 2—The Nature of Man
- I. The Nature of Man
- II. The Fall of Man
- III. The Seed of Rebellion Continues

Book 3—A Call to Faith and Obedience
- I. Abraham: The Father of Faith and Obedience
- II. Israel: Called to Be the People of God

Book 4—From Covenant to Kingdom
- I. Taking Possession of the Promises of God
- II. Establishing the Kingdom
- III. The Message of the Prophets
- IV. Restoring the Remnant of Israel

Book 5—The New Covenant
- I. The New Covenant
- II. The Person of Jesus Christ
- III. The Nature of Jesus Christ
- IV. The Humiliation of Jesus Christ

Book 6—Jesus Christ, Servant of God
    I.   Wounded for Our Transgressions
    II.   Bruised for Our Iniquities
    III.   Chastised for Our Peace
    IV.   Scourged for Our Healing

Book 7—The Exaltation of Christ
    I.   The Exaltation of Jesus Christ
    II.   Jesus and the Kingdom of God
           Summary

More Titles by Dr. Mark Hanby

▬ YOU HAVE NOT MANY FATHERS
"My son, give me your heart." So says the proverb, echoing the heart and passion of our Father in heaven. God has spiritual "dads" all over the world whom He has filled with wisdom, knowledge, compassion, and most of all, love for those young in the faith. You do not have to go through your life untrained and unloved; uncared for and forgotten. There are fathers in Christ who are waiting to pour all they have into your heart, as Elijah did for Elisha. "My son, give me your heart."
ISBN 1-56043-166-0

▬ YOU HAVE NOT MANY FATHERS STUDY GUIDE
ISBN 0-7684-2036-9

▬ THE HOUSE THAT GOD BUILT
Beyond whatever man can desire is a God-given pattern for the life of the Church. Here Dr. Hanby unfolds practical applications from the design of the Tabernacle that allow us to become the house God is building today.
ISBN 1-56043-091-5

▬ THE HOUSE THAT GOD BUILT STUDY GUIDE
ISBN 0-7684-2048-2

▬ THE RENEWING OF THE HOLY GHOST
Do you need renewal? Everything in the natural, from birds to blood cells, must either undergo a process of renewal or enter into death. Our spiritual life is no different. With this book, your renewal can begin today!
ISBN 1-56043-031-1

▬ ANOINTING THE UNSANCTIFIED
The anointing is more than a talented performance or an emotional response. In this book, Dr. Hanby details the essential ingredients of directional relationship that allow the Spirit of God to flow down upon the Body of Christ—and from us to the needs of a dying world.
ISBN 1-56043-071-0

▬ PERCEIVING THE WHEEL OF GOD
On the potter's wheel, a lump of clay yields to a necessary process of careful pressure and constant twisting. Similarly, the form of true faith is shaped by a trusting response to God in a suffering situation. This book offers essential understanding for victory through the struggles of life.
ISBN 1-56043-109-1

Available at your local Christian bookstore.

For more information and sample chapters, visit www.destinyimage.com